listen & play blues KEYBOARD

Listen then play the blues like it should be played!

This unique book and CD will give you the tools to transform the music you read into the way blues keyboard should sound.

- A new way to listen & learn to play the blues.
- Listen & learn to play traditional blues boogie, walking bass, funky chords, and melodies in authentic blues style.
- Listen & learn how to get your playing to sound genuine as you play blues standards.
- Easy to learn! Easy to play!

Dr. Bert Konowitz
Professor of Music
Teachers College, Columbia University

Copyright © MMII by Alfred Publishing Co., Inc.
All rights reserved. Printed in USA.
ISBN 0-7390-1669-5

Cover photo: © 2002 Kathryn Hollinrake/Masterfile
CD recorded and engineered by Jon Greathouse

contents

introducing the blues

listen & play the blues—the blues way

why…*listen & play blues*?

Early blues generally was not written down nor published in a book like this one. Players and singers created the blues by describing, in music, the world as they experienced it. As a result, their emotions were expressed using performance nuances that defy traditional musical notation. Just as the blues style initially was passed on by *listening* and *imitating*, the **Listen & Play** method is similar to that tradition.

what is *listen & play blues*?

This unique book and CD will give you the tools to transform the music that you read into the way it should sound when played. Written music offers the notes, but it may not completely tell you how to perform them. Playing the blues in an authentic manner requires specific techniques that can be difficult to notate. However, you can achieve this by combining *note reading* along with *listening to a recording* of how it is supposed to sound. Once and for all, the **Listen & Play** approach puts an end the often-heard lament, "I'm reading the notes correctly, but why doesn't it sound like the blues?"

Photo: Institute of Jazz Studies

In the late 1920s **Count Basie** found himself surrounded by the blues. For the rest of his life the blues would be at the heart of everything he did.

how does *listen & play blues* work?

This book is divided into two main sections:

part I: getting the sound & feel of the blues

The basic musical techniques that create the blues sound are introduced in a slow, sequential manner. These techniques are presented in a way that make them clearly understandable and ready for practice. An easy-to-play original piece that highlights the technique just presented follows immediately.

To create an authentic sounding blues performance, follow the **Listen & Play** approach. We recommend that you follow these three steps to achieve quick success:

1. Listen to the CD as you read along from the printed page (track numbers are indicated adjacent to each example and piece).
2. Play the track again as you play along ***with*** the CD. Repeat as necessary.
3. Play ***without*** the CD as a soloist. Your goal should be to sound like the CD.

All the warm-up exercises in Part I are recorded at a slow tempo. This offers the player an opportunity to learn each new skill with ease.

Tracks 6, 11, 15, 20, 25 and 29 are full-length performance compositions recorded at two different tempos. First, the composition is played at a slower speed to allow one to learn the piece well. The second performance is the true speed at which the performance will sound best. The remaining compositions in Part I are recorded once at normal tempo.

part II: spotlight on solos

A variety of standard blues compositions stand side by side with new, original pieces. These solos are specially arranged using the basic musical techniques that you learned to play in Part I of the book.

Each solo is recorded once at normal tempo, and it is recommended that you follow the **Listen & Play** approach as indicated above. Now you have an opportunity to build a blues repertoire that will bring you and your audience great enjoyment.

a short history of the blues

Through the years, the blues style has stood as a basic foundation around which jazz and rock have developed. As a result of the evolution of jazz and rock, the blues has taken on many different meanings for different people. To some, it is a specific type of chord progression in which blues singers offer musical messages of deep personal feelings, mostly dealing with love, jealousy, sadness and despair. The same blues chord progression also serves as the starting point from which instrumentalists create improvised melodies or written-out compositions such as "St. Louis Blues." Others propose that the blues is a mood, a style of performance, a state of mind.

Perhaps the beauty of the blues is that it is a musical experience through which all people—skilled musicians or untrained music lovers—can make or find a personal statement. Whether performed slow or fast, sad or happy, with words, or on handmade or professionally produced instruments, by a soloist or a large musical group, the blues continues to survive many years of musical change because it touches something very basic in each of us.

Born out of the roots of slavery in America, the blues has since been performed worldwide. The true bedrock of the most influential blues is found in the Mississippi Delta. Later, as the blues merged with European musical forms, performers, ranging from solo guitarists with no formal musical training to blues singers performing with sophisticated backup bands, used the musical elements of the blues to create a wealth of musical repertoire.

Photo: Institute of Jazz Studies

W. C. Handy is considered one of the true "inventors" of the blues. Late in his life he dedicated his career to publishing and promoting African-American music. His most famous composition was "St. Louis Blues" (page 40). Composed in 1914, this classic has been recorded by many great blues performers, including Bessie Smith and Louis Armstrong.

From the last part of the 19th century through the periods of World War I, the Depression of the 1920s and 1930s, the World War II era of the 1940s and right up to today, the great names of jazz and rock have created and performed the blues. An all-star list would include Big Bill Broonzy, Leadbelly, Ma Rainey and Bessie Smith, Albert King, W. C. Handy, Louis Armstrong, Chuck Berry, Ray Charles, Elvis Presley and Muddy Waters. The creative works of Count Basie, Duke Ellington, Benny Goodman and other swing bands of the 1930s and 1940s; the eventual development of the styles of Charlie Parker and the beboppers; and John Coltrane and Wynton Marsalis, all reflect the techniques and feelings of the blues. Jazz, rock, and pop music of today still contain many ingredients of the blues. The blues style will probably live forever.

the blues progression

The blues progression (a sequence of chords) is a basic musical form that is used by blues, jazz and rock performers to create and improvise blues songs and/or instrumental melodies. The blues progression usually consists of 12 measures using three basic chords.

In the key of C major, these three chords are:

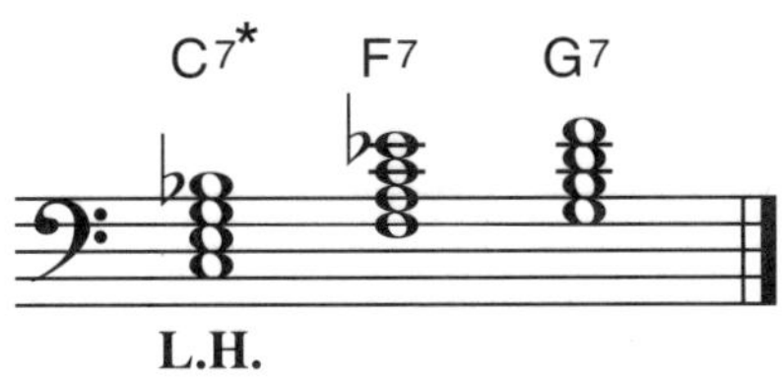

These three chords are generally organized in the following sequence to create the standard 12-bar blues progression. Knowing this progression will help you understand the structure of blues performance.

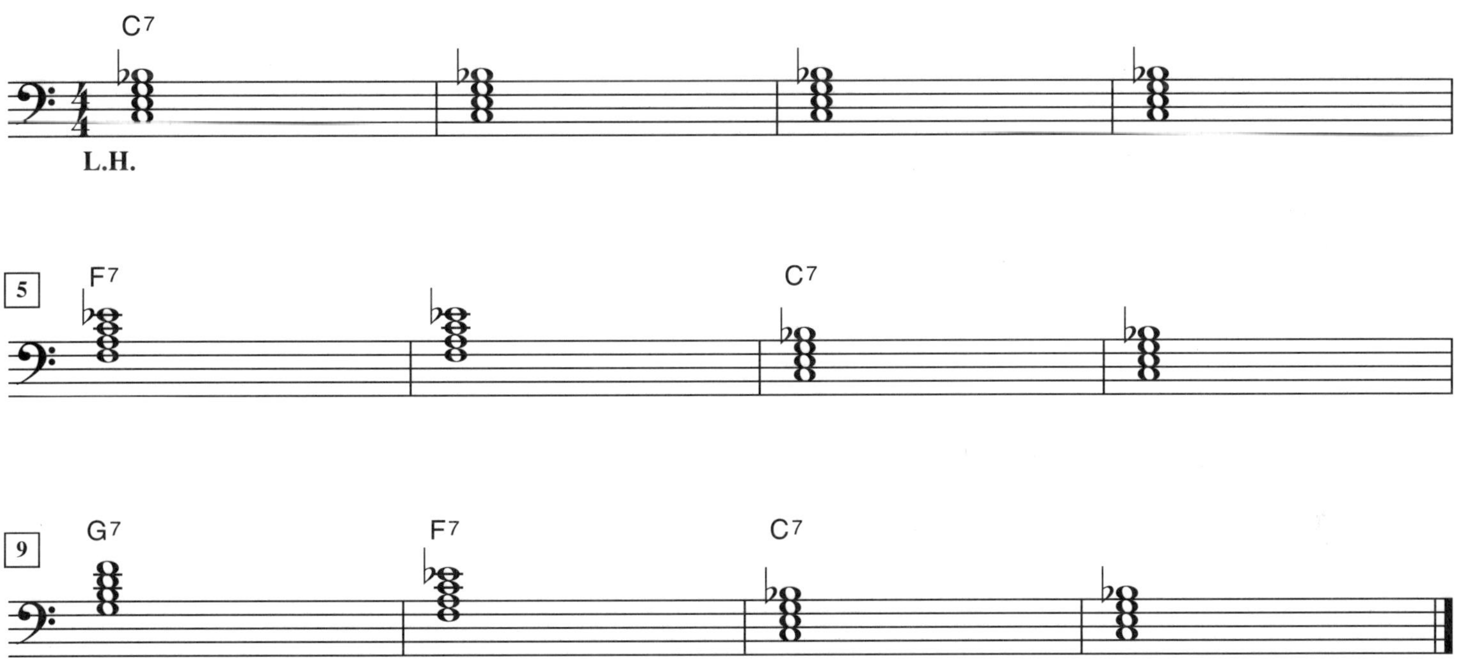

Track 1

blues progression warm-up

Listen to the blues progression above and memorize the chord sequence.

Play and learn the "C^7," "F^7" and "G^7" chords ***without*** the CD so that you can perform them easily in tempo.

Play along ***with*** the CD, repeating several times.

*See the chord chart on page 48.

part I: getting the sound & feel of the blues

play

the standard 12-bar blues progression

Warm up to the blues as you **Listen & Play.**

(Swing style)*

listen & play

Track 2

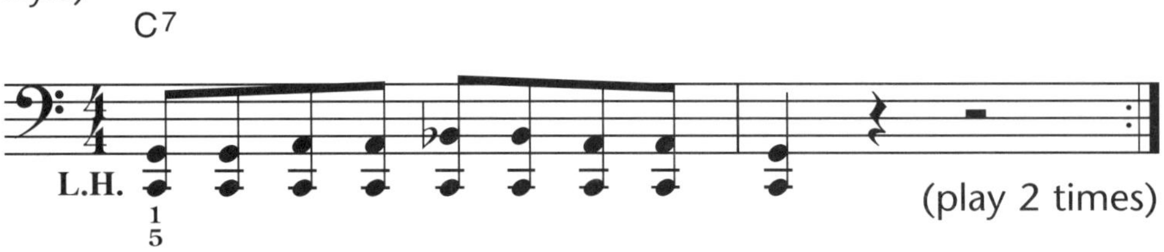

(play 2 times)

listen & play

Track 3

(play 2 times)

listen & play

Track 4

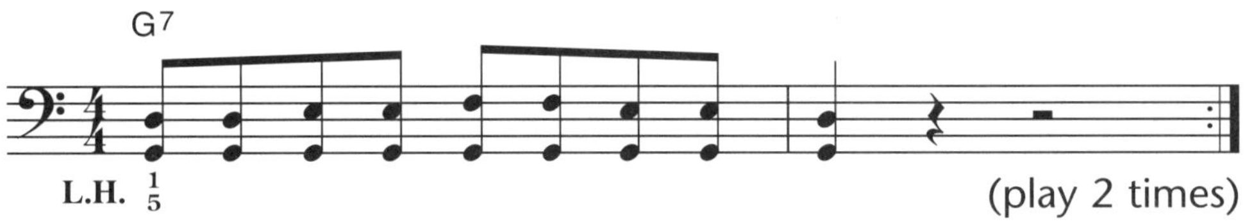

(play 2 times)

*The blues is generally played in a swing style (=).

Track 5

listen & play

the blues progression

This is the standard chord progression for most blues.

Track 6.1, Practice Tempo
Track 6.2, Performance Tempo

listen & play

shuffle blues

*In some cases the standard 12-bar blues progression will be extended beyond 12 measures to enhance the ending of a composition.

play
blues rhythm with a steady feel

listen & play
Track 7

listen & play
Track 8

listen & play
Track 9

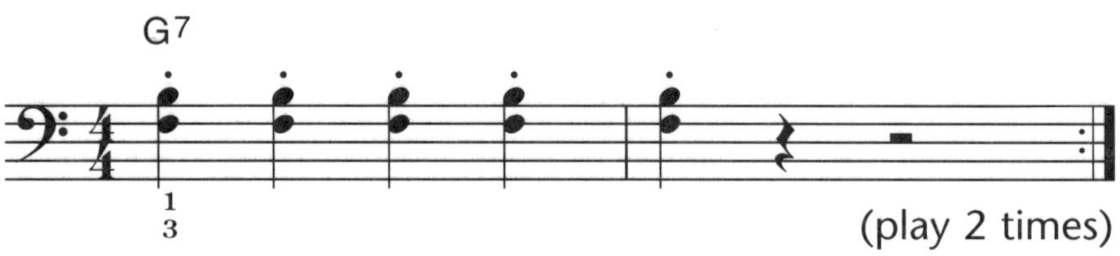

Track 10
listen & play
the blues progression (slightly altered)

The second measure of the blues progression is occasionally changed from a C^7 to an F^7 for variety.

Track 11.1, Practice Tempo
Track 11.2, Performance Tempo

listen & play

Blind Lemon's blues

Blind Lemon Jefferson was one of the most famous of the original country blues singers. His original blues songs and performances captured the intense emotions and values of the early blues days of America.

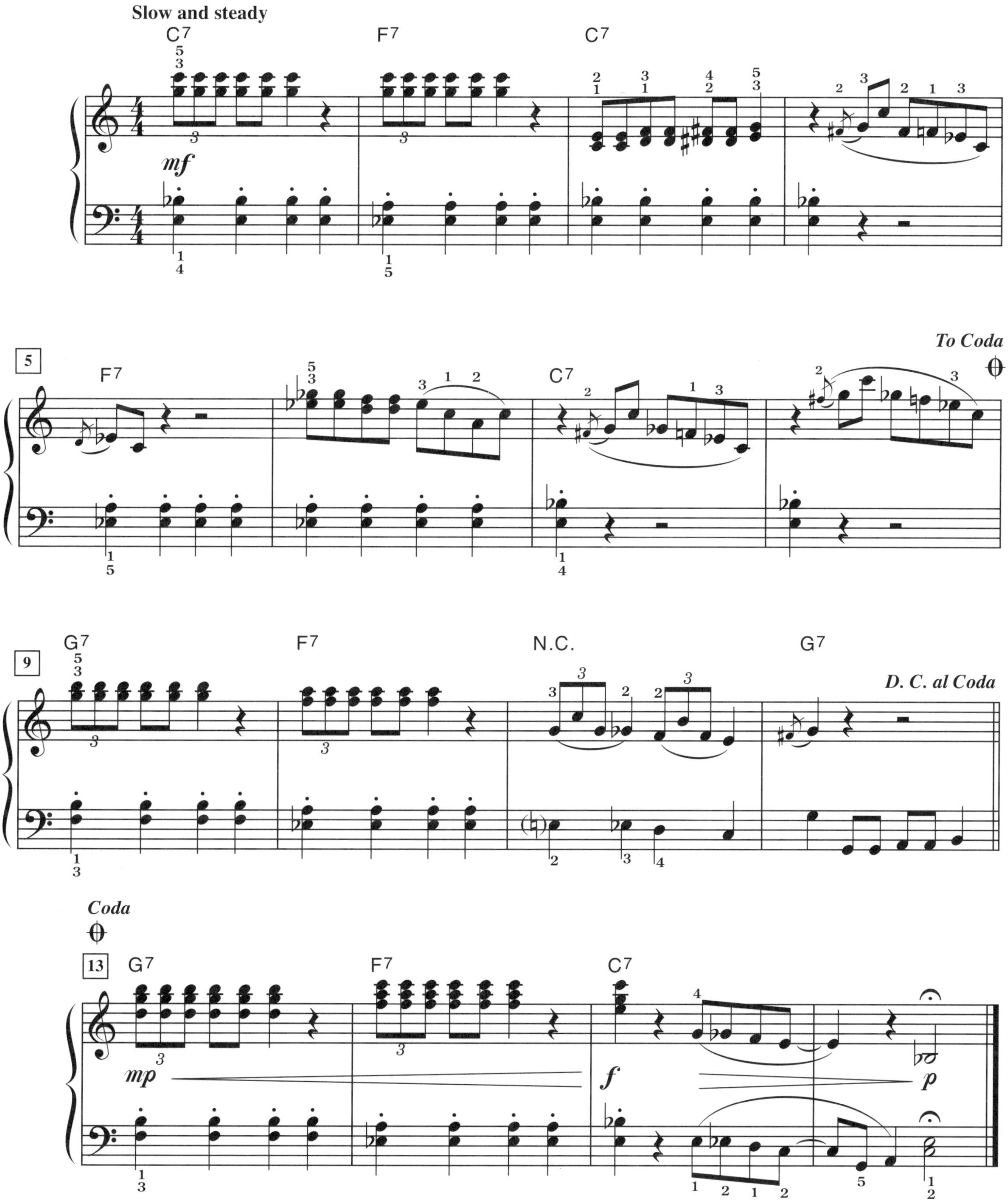

Here is how a slightly different 12-bar blues progression is expanded into a 32-bar performance piece.

Track 12

listen & play

just chuggin' along

14 F7 C F7
18 C
p
21 G7 F7 D7 G C C7
mf
25 D7 G7 C7 F7
29 C N.C. D7 G7 C
p
mf
f

Here is a salute to one of the great innovators of jazz. The legendary Jelly Roll Morton was a great pianist, composer and arranger who combined the early blues style and feel with the more formal ragtime.

Track 13

listen & play

Jelly Roll's blues

14
mp
17
F7
C7
21
G7
F7
D7
G7
C
25
C7
mf
mp
C
F
C
f

play
blues melody with the blues scale

The blues scale creates an authentic sound that *is* the blues. The accents add to the blues feel.

listen & play
Track 14

Track 15.1, Practice Tempo
Track 15.2, Performance Tempo

listen & play
the Ray Charles blues progression

Ray Charles added excitement to the blues with his emotional and gospel-influenced singing and piano playing.

listen & play

Track 16

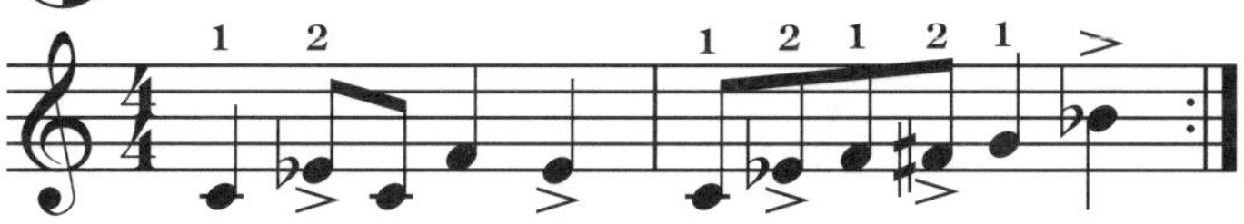

(play 2 times)

listen & play

Track 17

(play 2 times)

listen & play

Track 18

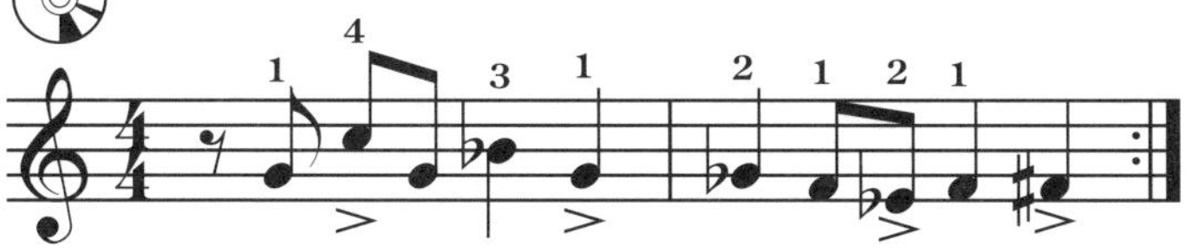

(play 2 times)

listen & play

Track 19

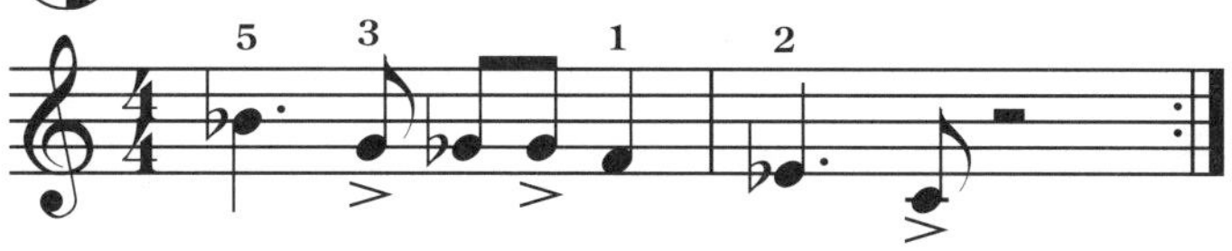

(play 2 times)

Track 20.1, Practice Tempo
Track 20.2, Performance Tempo

listen & play

the Lady Day (Billie Holiday) blues

The great saxophonist Lester Young nicknamed Billie Holiday "Lady Day."
She is a legend in a long line of blues singers, including Bessie Smith and Ella Fitzgerald.

Track 21

listen & play

Jackson Square

Jackson Square is a part of the history of blues and jazz when it was first performed in New Orleans.

17
Cm7
mp
21
Fm7
Gm7
Cm7
mf-p
25
mp
29
Cm7/G
8va
slowly
f
p

play

blues melody with crushed notes

Crushed notes (𝅘𝅥𝅮) are played simultaneously with the following note and released immediately.

listen & play

Track 22

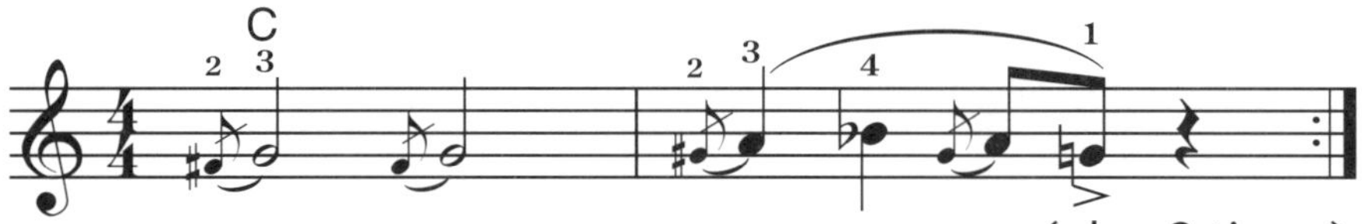

(play 2 times)

listen & play

Track 23

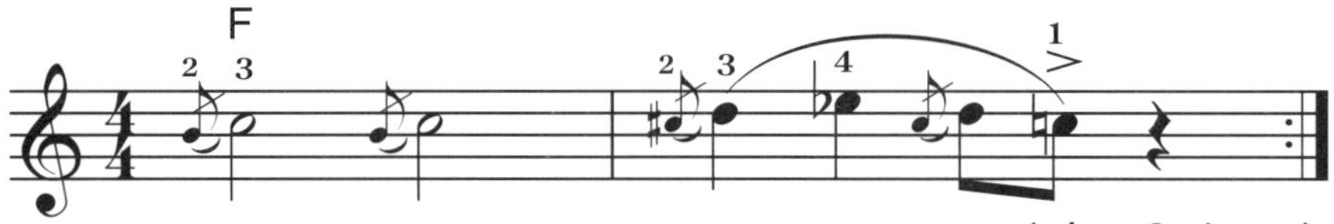

(play 2 times)

listen & play

Track 24

(play 2 times)

Track 25.1, Practice Tempo
Track 25.2, Performance Tempo

listen & play

Satchmo's blues

Louis "Satchmo" Armstrong's musical contributions as a trumpet player, improviser and singer are considered among the most influential in jazz and the blues.

play
blues melody with tremolo

Tremolo: Alternating rapidly between two notes or chords.

listen & play

Track 26

listen & play

Track 27

listen & play

Track 28

Track 29.1, Practice Tempo
Track 29.2, Performance Tempo

listen & play
the W.C. Handy blues

W. C. Handy crowned himself "Father of the Blues." He wrote "St. Louis Blues" and his "Memphis Blues" is the first blues composition ever to be published.

Track 30

listen & play

Basie's blues train

William "Count" Basie introduced the walking bass (left hand in measures 5–14) in his performances.

17
Cm7
F7
Cm7
21
F7
C
25
G7
F7
C7
mf gradually slower
29
f very slow
8va lower

play left-hand blues boogie

listen & play

Track 31

listen & play

Track 32

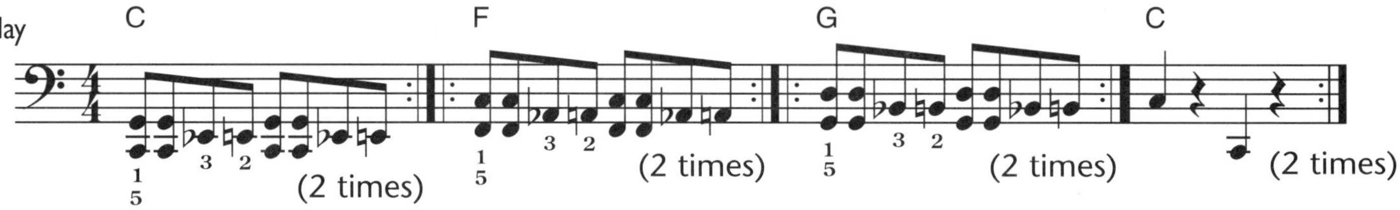

listen & play

Track 33

Track 34

listen & play

the Meade Lux Lewis boogie

The excitement of boogie-woogie began with early blues and extends into the rock music of today. Meade Lux Lewis was one of the most creative pianists using this energetic rhythmic style.

9
G7
F7
C
Fine
13
C7
17
F7
C
21
G7
F7
C
25
C
F7
C
F7
D. C. al Fine

play right-hand blues patterns

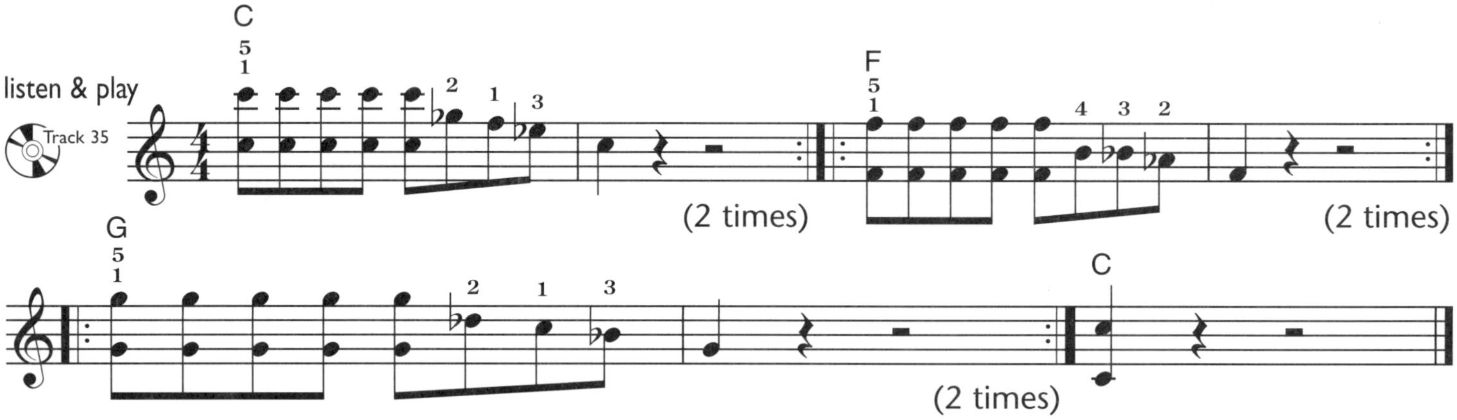

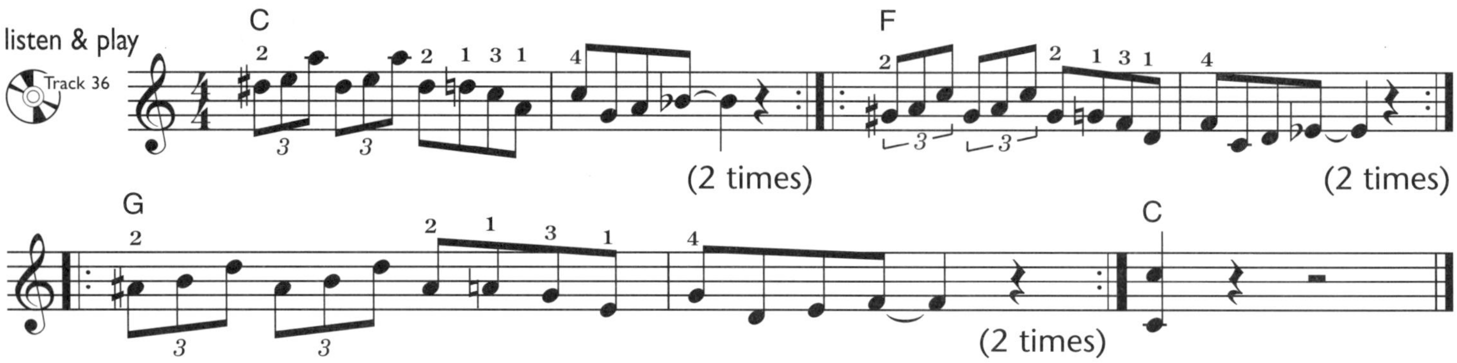

Track 37

listen & play

salute to Mary Lou Williams

Pianist, composer and arranger Mary Lou Williams was a child prodigy who became a legendary musician by the time she was a teenager. She used boogie left-hand patterns with repetitive right-hand blues patterns in her imaginative playing.

9
G
F
C
Fine
f
13
F7
C7
mp
p
17
G7
C
mp
21
F
C7
8va
f
p
25
G7
C
D. C. al Fine
f

Track 38

listen & play

come on down

17
C
F
F♯°7
ff
mf
21
C/G
C/E
E♭°7
D7
D♭7
C7
mp
25
C/G
C/E
E♭
D7
G7(♭5)
F
C
f
29
C/G
C
mf
f
8va lower

play

blues lag-a-long rhythm—using your ear

Lag-a-long: A note or notes played slightly late or after the beat. This is often referred to as "playing behind the beat."

listen & play

Track 39

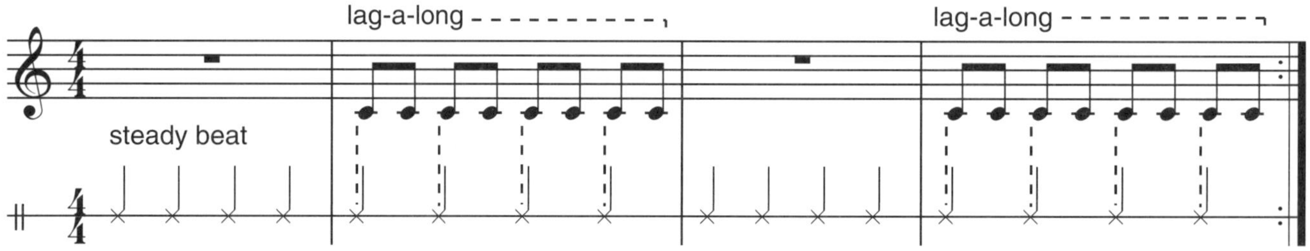

listen & play

Track 40

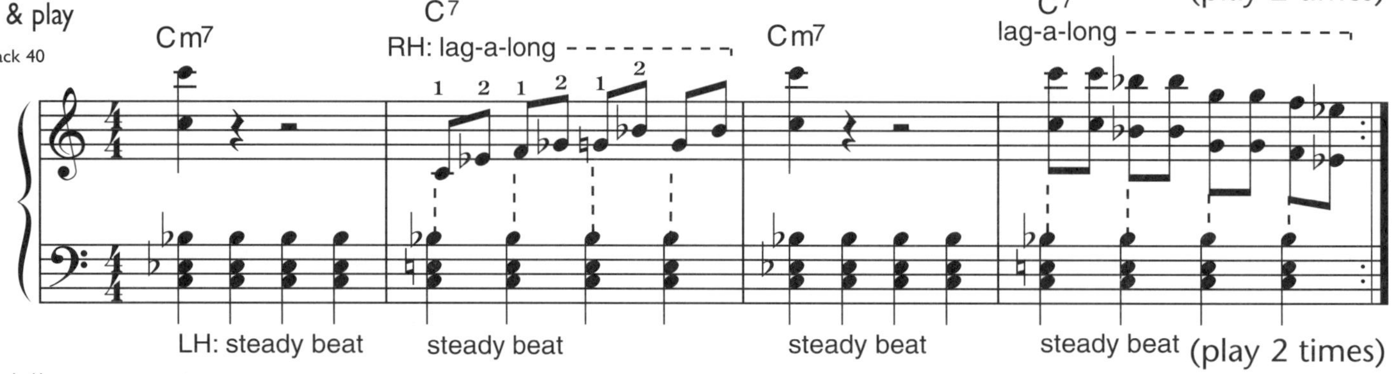

Track 41

listen & play

the Errol Garner blues

Errol Garner's trademark of his unique piano style is his playing of left-hand chords on the beat while the right hand is performed slightly behind the beat (i.e., lag-a-long).

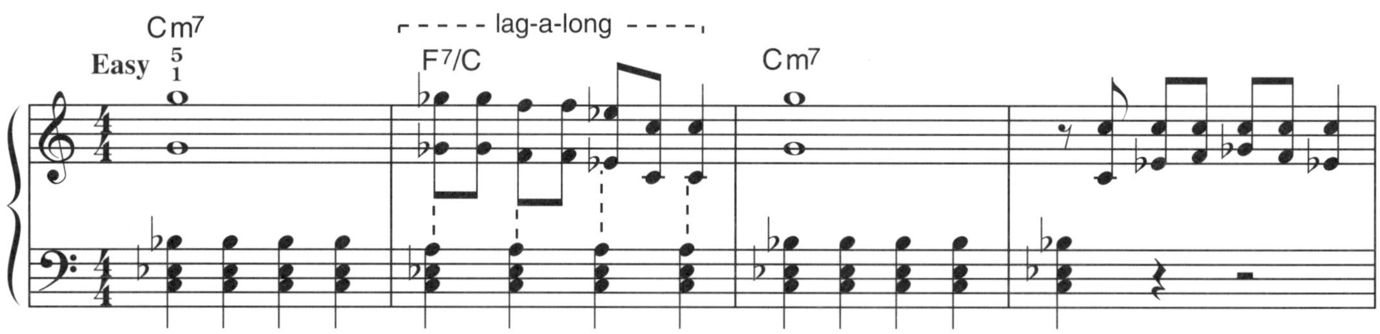

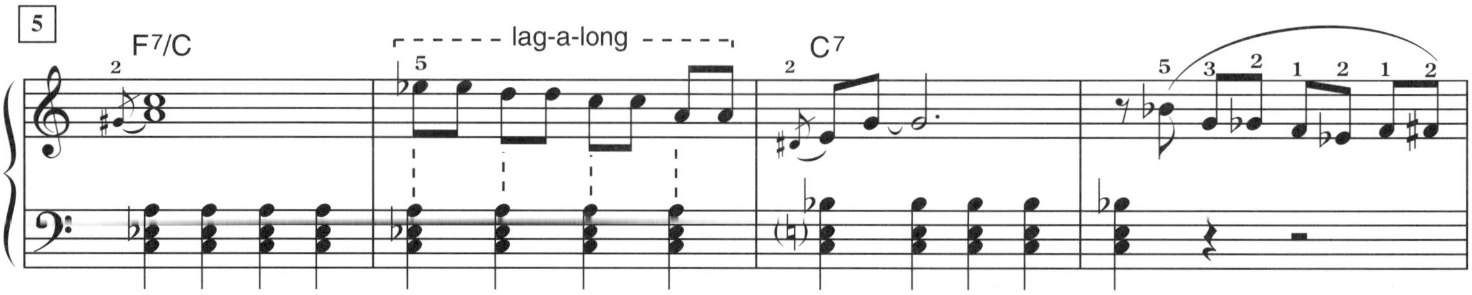

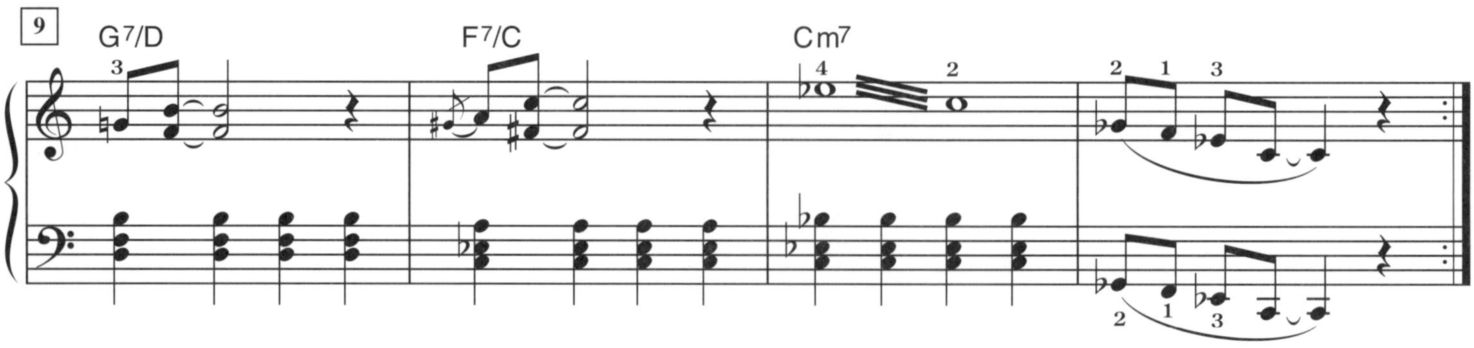

Track 42

listen & play

slow goin'

play
walking bass

The walking bass is used in blues playing to lay down a strong, solid beat.

listen & play
Track 43

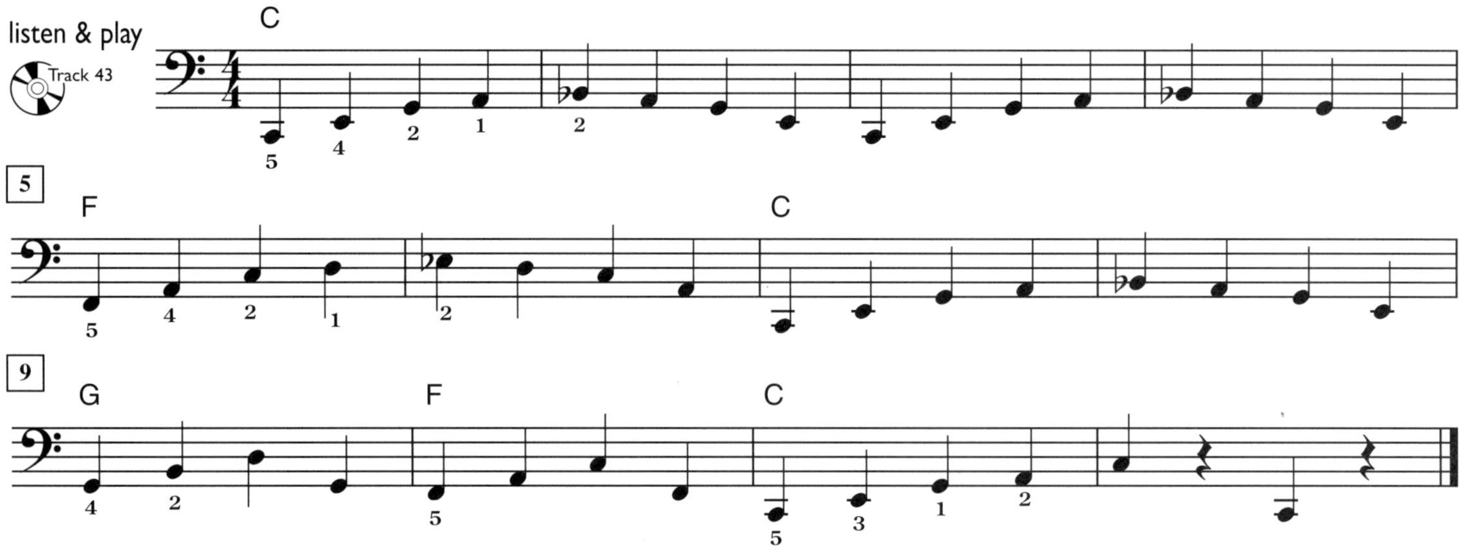

Track 44

listen & play
walkin' the blues

Track 45

listen & play

time for Jimmy Blanton

Jimmy Blanton was a creative bass player with Duke Ellington who performed solid walking bass lines.

part II: spotlight on solos

Here's your chance to perform on center stage. Each of the solos in Part II has been uniquely created to give you and your audience a special blues experience. Use the skills previously learned to make this a spotlight event.

Track 46

listen & play

the saints go marching in blues

Traditional
arr. by Bert Konowitz

17
C/G
E7/G♯
Am
G7/B
To Coda
C
mf
f - p - f
repeat 3 times
21
C7
25
F7
C7
29
G7
lag-a-long
F7
C
mf - p - f
play 3 times
D. C. al Coda
Coda

Track 47

listen & play

blues riff

Bert Konowitz

C7
lag-a-long
F7
C7
F7
lag-a-long
C7
G7
F7
C7
lag-a-long
Dm7
G7
C
Cm
Dm
G7
D. C. al Fine

Track 48

listen & play

Ja-Da

Bob Carleton
arr. by Bert Konowitz

17
C
A7/E
D7/F♯
G7/F
C/E
21
C7/E
A7/C♯
D7
G
25
C/E
Cm/E♭
D7
G
C/E
Cm/E♭
A♭7
G7
29
C
E7
Am
D7
G7
C
mp
pp

Track 49

listen & play

ballad of the blues

Bert Konowitz

F7
lag-a-long
Cm/G
G7
Cm
Fm7
D♭7
Cm7
A♭7
G7
Cm
slower
p
f
mp
pp

Track 50

listen & play

St. Louis blues

W. C. Handy
arr. by Bert Konowitz

17
Cm
21
C
lag-a-long
F7
C
25
F7
C
29
D7
G7
C

Track 51

listen & play

left-turn boogie

Bert Konowitz

C
F7
C
A♭7
G7
C
play 3 times f - p - f

Track 52

listen & play

Americana blues

Bert Konowitz

17
C7
F7
A7
p
21
D7
G7
C
mf
f
25
mf
mp
29
F7
C

(Nobody Knows the Trouble I've Seen)

(Go Tell It on the Mountain)
49
C
G7
C
mf
53
E7/B
Am
F7
F♯°7
mp
57
F7
G7
C
C
Slower
mf
mp
(America, the Beautiful)
61
F
B7
C/E
B♭
A7
a tempo
D7
G7
C7
slowly
mf
freely
f
p

chord chart

Chord symbols are used to help keyboard players add harmony to the melody and fake the left-hand accompaniments. Here are some of the basic chords, many of which are used in this book.

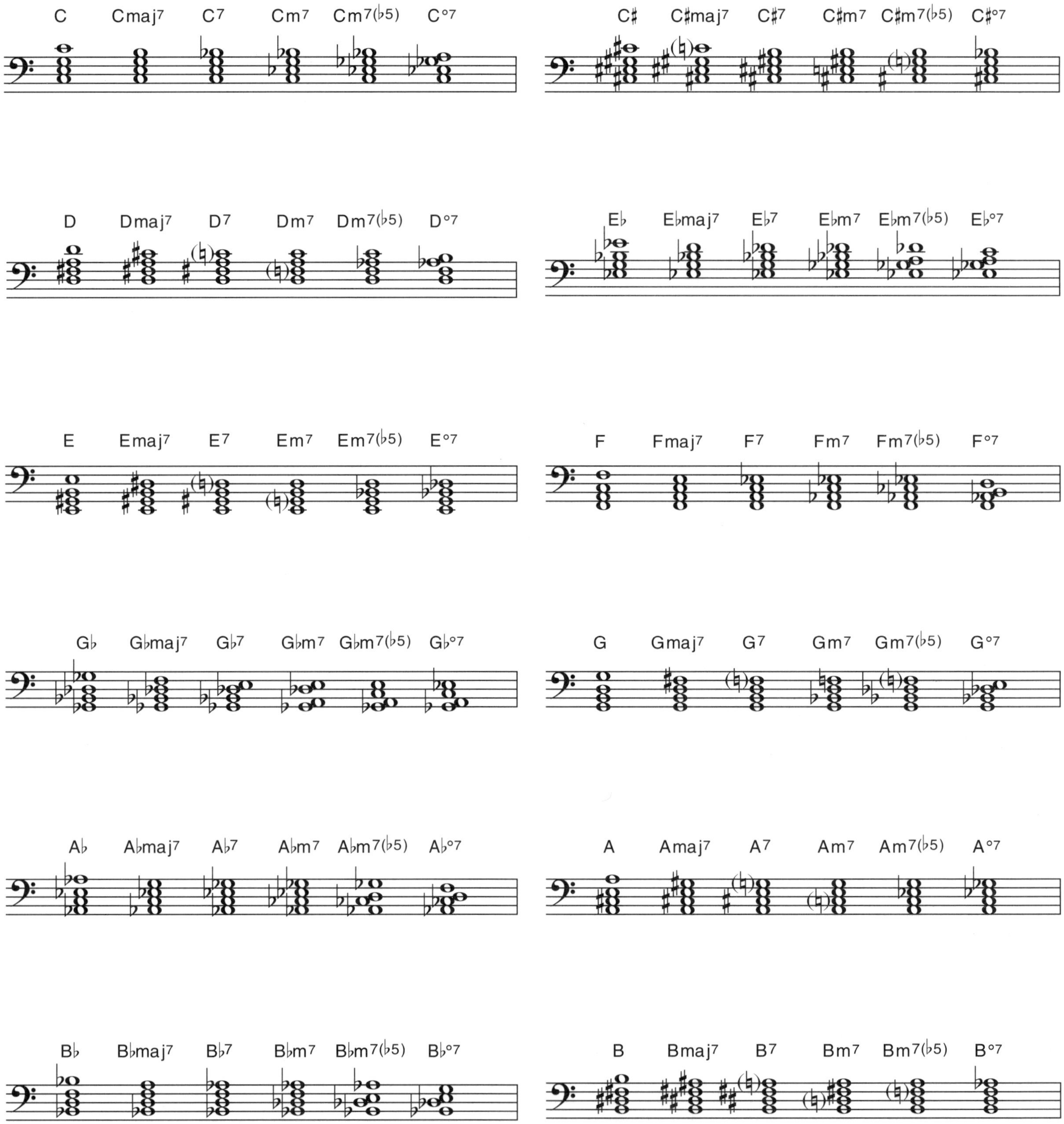